VIA Folios 138

Season of Subtraction

Season of Subtraction

PROSE POEMS

Michelle Reale

BORDIGHERA PRESS

Library of Congress Control Number: 2019933624

These poems are dedicated to my Aunt Jeanne Marie,
with much love and gratitude.

Cover art by Svetlana Rumak
Places Where Our Hearts Return Again and Again

Printed in the United States.

Published by
BORDIGHERA PRESS
John D. Calandra Italian American Institute
25 West 43rd Street, 17th Floor
New York, NY 10036

VIA FOLIOS 138
ISBN 978-1-59954-136-5

CONTENTS

This is the season of subtraction
When what goes away is what stays.

—CHARLES WRIGHT, "A Journal of One Significant Season"

Oh, how we want
to be taken
And changed
Want to be mended
By what we enter.

—JORIE GRAHAM, "Erosion"

PROLOGUE

When the dream occurs as it often does, it is always the same. Someone hands me a child, an infant, still and quiet. My eyes take in the contours of its soft, downy head and move down to its fragile and pulsating chest, mottled pink. The little arms are well muscled. They stretch upward as though already understanding what will be beyond their reach. The toenails are pink, like fresh, harvested pearls, and the feet curl in on themselves. From the delicate and tiny shoulder blades sprout the buds of little wings, finely feathered and more than just ornamental. They seem to signal, catch me; find me.

Or let me go for good.

TESSERAE

The bands of cohabitation were *fait accompli*. The street names either boasted or warned of biblical plagues, a portent of strife. The foothold of the craggy-necked children of slaves was indisputable; no one thought to hold a grudge. Witness the hoarding of the apples, a carrot, the rare orange when it appeared. But generosity reigned like a king. The one-sided accounts did no justice to mere survival. The crumbling red brick houses where bathtub gin and whisky was brewed were marked with Mr. Johnson's yellow "X". A courtesy for those who were so inclined. Those born extreme south of Naples patrolled the streets that were covered in asbestos and dust, made tallies for the mothers of the sons who were out loafing. Clemency, always a strong trait amongst those who told tales on the crumbling front steps, attached to dejected wooden porches, was more than just rumor. The old-before-her-time Sicilian dragged her misshapen feet in soft felt slippers along Locust, collecting rent in change. Later, she'd order her husband to bed and open the cellar door of her house on the corner. Her son would sit and smoke. Calculate the reliability of attraction and count the minutes a second at a time. She'd give advice in crude dialect and fractured English, then serve a nickel's worth of whiskey in squat shot glasses clean as a virgin's conscience.

EATING YOUR SEED CORN

Georgette crepe with a velvet trim in navy blue. Desire, like a fist down the throat. The swish against the silk stockings. This is the coming to the edge. A look like a lock on a chain link fence and Holy Scripture at even intervals throughout the day could not hold back the force. The tinted distance becomes a chamber in two stages: what exists now, in this moment and whatever came before. The unlucky are destined to never know. The backdrop of the high street, the well-shod feet that traverse the new course of daily life on the cracked paving stones might tell one story. Lies on black, furtive breath, anger bleeding, love repeated might tell another, more obscured version. Free spirits, suffragettes and the newly arrived make misdirected and fanciful forays into the abyss. They know it, but they march ahead anyway

REVOLVER

The shot arrow soars through the thickness of tradition, piercing generations of order, expectation. We imagine she is unsuspecting or complicit. She may be docile, though he encourages her with the side eye, hard to resist. Let's say they meet in the room with the hammered cathedral ceiling. Let's say he lights her cigarette, noting the chipped red nail polish on her sensible fingers. Let's imagine she dismisses the smell of solvent on his clothes, the cracks on his fingertips as the type of inconveniences all humans must endure. He thinks green is the most beautiful color and he tells her so. She squares her sturdy shoulders, steps over the threshold into a bright day with him. Already she feels stirring, traces the arterial routes of commitment, the essence of revolving doors. By evening, they are shrouded in quivering, silky darkness. They shiver at the sight of their own shadows; the heaviness of what they know.

RECURRENCE

You are encased in ice. You are barefoot and blue, in snow. For variation you are hunched and clinging to a high wall so smooth, you have nothing to hold on to. For variation you are surrounded by water, wet and hunched, hugging your own knees as if giving birth to yourself. Later, your arms put themselves to use, paddling like a mechanism into the future; no user's manual required. You remain steady, and manage the mutable smile, the lips cracking at the effort. You grip the blooming flowers, bruised but still beautiful with your balsa wood fingers. At the time, you could not know that the vision you see as with a greased retina, the fleshy burden of the future: my father, in this garden, growing vulnerable things and coaxing the grass into a paradise of chlorophyll.

A jagged stone nesting in the valley of his parched throat.

THE BIRDS, HOW THEY CIRCLE

The breath is a miasma on the neck, a growing and alive thing. The breath that burns, the disinterested look that says *What about it?* It was the difference that mesmerizes: the cut of the suit jacket, the jaunt of the hat, peculiar in a man so young. The misunderstandings and miscalculations of tongues heavy as lead, making future plans in a language neither could speak. The nose twitches at the thought: scripture read at the breakfast table like a knife to the already serrated heart. Pressed against the dirt, or the brocade sofa in a room with drapes so heavy those with a prying eye or a strong wind could not penetrate them. Afterwards, the cawing of predatory birds sway in and out of formation. This is what we know: that only caged birds need or require our attention.

TETRAHEDRON

If she avoids him, it is with good reason: a man is a fetter, all thick iron links and smelling like hot blood. She stops taking the steps, two at a time; braces herself when jostled on the street, pulling her wool coat like a protective web around her. She meets the eyes of those who stare like sentries. What might he say? He held her as one might a pillow across the face of one you could not live without. Oxygen is a luxury. When all else fails, invent a new language, initiate others without their knowledge. Things are bound to come together at some point. All the new words will have a theme: relinquishment and deficit. His will be ignorance and rationalization. Enunciated in just the right way, words can start a war or spark a pleasant conversation. Does your mouth betray you? Not yet? *It will.* The animal in you suffers. By which I mean to say, it claws its way into you like a somnambulant on its way to a reckoning. It is the fire starters who never have the decency to look away.

EDGEWISE

She slips into life in a room; banal. But because we lack the details we crave, we hope our collective imaginations do not betray us. We can be romantic about it if we want to. The mother labors easily, mouth taught as a frayed nerve. She suspends belief in the last moments, but quickly catches herself. It is real (define real), though it also has the essence of funhouse to it, too. She finds herself in a scenario she swears she once glimpsed in a dream or one that her mother may have divined on a cold, starless night in the old country. There is a table of Formica; the tabletop pattern is not important at this moment, but it will be a detail hard to grasp many years hence. A lamp ringed in silky fringe, the shade a cardiac red, casting a rosy, though cold glow. The woman who assists her puffs her small cheeks as if she herself comes as close to death as she will ever be. Her large hands are like claws, opening and closing as if practicing. Everyone is sliding headfirst into the new reality. In her arms, the woman rubs the baby into existence, the muffled cry, small and inconsequential. On Locust Street, a man feels a pain in his side like a hot poker. He wipes his brow. His wife warms milk in a pan. They exchange no words. The dinner dishes soak in the porcelain sink where, uncharacteristically, she will leave them until morning. But first, she turns the key in the lock at midnight; still unaware.

UNSEEN

Some secrets masquerade as white silk, with gold filigree buttons. Some you have to work harder for, like pitching a shovel into solid ground, turning the gritty dirt over and over. In one home, a family sits in a room, together, but separate, all ossified bone and frayed seams. The radio broadcasts to the air. In another, an infant wails, throwing her tiny arms into the air as if in exquisite triumph. Her mother will roll her hair, powder her prominent clavicle, and paint her toenails. Eventually she calls the moon down from the velvet sky. Heats the glass bottle on the ring of blue flame.

PRIMOGENITURE

Curiosity like flames that lick the face with no reasonable defense against the lack, the striving for what or who, has yet to be named. Silence can be both blessing and vice for the ones who will take your birthright to the grave. How they dressed you in lace, with a ruffle or two in strategic places. How they compared your features to theirs; the slight cast of the eye, the contour of the cheek; the irregularity of coloring; the stubborn streak mercifully skipping a generation. Contemplate the coerced silence into keeping what you know clothed in heavy robes like a fallen priest. You grind your teeth in your sleep. You call other women *sisters* and *mine*. The near apocalyptic urge to know seeps from every pore. It creates a critical mass in which your feet will be firmly planted in place for years to come.

LIQUIDATED

Grief like a fist in the face. You gather your skirts about you and contemplate the care you took. Rejection cracks the spine in a number of places. Much energy will be spent trying to calm the thick veined heart muscle in the pulpy chest wall. You are tethered by a wisp of recognition, the fragile DNA, coiled within in you, that you share. You remember the shape of the eyes, the cleft in the chin, the length of the nose, like that of a dictator who has seen better days. The man who is your father keeps his heart behind barbed wire, obscures malice, plays at benevolence. His raspy whisper begs and pleads. *Go away.* Any connection, if not already extinguished will be dead on arrival. *All in good time.*

PROXIMITY

Down the square tiled aisles and across from the soda fountain, a young girl holds stands, holding the hand of her mother with a mouth like a red gash. You walk softly on your toes, the way you have been taught to do in similar, delicate situations. You make careful note of the store displays, make note that time seems to have stood as still as the mother and daughter, who seem to be buying nothing, their hands empty except for the skin between them. The color of the toys is bright. The row upon row of candy promises sweetness or decay. *You try to resist.* The mother whispers to her daughter, serious-like as if reciting a decade of the rosary. She leans down, her mouth close to her ear. There is a moment of agony, of the possible breach of a threshold. Exit with one quick look over the shoulder. Make careful note of being seen.

INCENDIARY

Denial is muscular. Hope a wisp of a thing. Pat each of your children on the head, but stop yourself before you go too far. Your wife washes the same dish over and over again in the grip of dread. Repetitive motion has its place. The cadence of your voices rises and the children scatter upstairs, place their tongues against frosted window panes thick with ice, a boon to the parched, the thirsty. Your mouth turns dry with what cannot be said out loud and the heart is made of bile. We swallow our teeth for all we wish we could say. You are a flinty thing, rotating in the orbit of the one who wants only to be found. Five or six children, sodden thick with fear. Their names, a legacy of ancient and feudal heritage. But outside a potential surprise around every corner: a fuse just waiting for someone to strike a match.

PRESCRIPTIVE

Steady the rusted anvil, place the shoe sole side up and rip the heel. Peer into the abyss. First, being a shoemaker is no catastrophe. Second, relish the view you have from a large storefront window and a plumb position on the avenue. Remember, others can see in, too. Third, express the turning inside out of antiquated footwear as a reinvigorated art form— something out of time, but in fashion again. In matters of the heart, though, try not to flay the skin of your own as you contemplate vice and virtue. You are no Giotto and the timeless sky is not your canvass. Stick to basics: buff the leather. Jolt yourself into a new awareness. Take things into account outside of your ledger: like the child who walks with a stone in each shoe; an aproned servant in a disembodied palace, forever closed for repairs.

ALL BUT THE DEAD AND DYING

In the last dregs of winter, the birds were still making their southern migration. *A bad sign.* That year I scanned faces on the street, made features fit even when implausibility stared right back at me. I was in and out of my own way, and made promises of whatever was within my own power. The notion that I could still discover something was still present, but it had a shelf life—like the last thing in the refrigerator that you've passed over too many times—until you were starving. The hazards inherent digging up the past is that it is, of course, never really the past. Instead, though dormant, it is patient possessing just enough nuances to your animated engagement to keep the dead in repose. Until the time, when it comes, is just right.

GENUS

Temporality was auspicious. We had blown our heritage to mythic proportions, believed we could redress sins that we inherited, marking us like scar tissue. We recognized this in one another. Blood memory has no expiration date, but it requires culling the truth. We were ill-equipped, all thumbs. I always wanted to ask: when you held the mirror to your face, what did you see? Why be surprised by the displacement of features in a familiar landscape? It wasn't my fault that I didn't know your name, your blood type, that you called your grandmother *Mother*. Or that you called your father like a prayer to the deaf. How many moons waxed gibbous since I stacked my longing against your fervent wishes for every season, year after year? Global nodes are blinking. I answer the call locally. There is an old reality that I have become used to and it smells like sour wine.

Show me the way.

SEQUELAE

How quickly we'd all forgotten the shadows the eclipse cast, all eyebrow moons on cracked concrete. Omens sometimes come as natural phenomena, but only to those who pay attention and are willing to take them personally. *I've learned a thing or two.* Standing right in front of me I take in your form like an apparition, the soft cheek, the hands bearing rings, the wrist, a bangle. The alchemy is slow, but builds momentum. I am in alibi mode. I self-protect. I shed tears that scald my cheeks and am without defense. My father stands to the side, searches your features for his father and finds them. Your sister breathes the word sister into the air around us and we are intoxicated. We are all falling down now. The revenant watches from a dark corner. We raise our glasses anyway. Our breath hangs, hesitant in the thick air around us. All the things we ever wanted to say.

WHAT MAKES YOU CRY

Is often temporary. Set your skirt on fire and first you will bless the warmth, until you realize it burns you. Every path will have a different outcome. Chart your course. *Signal a pause in the turmoil.* Play the long game. Let's life the girl curled into herself, only 16, with a heart made of glass. In someone's kitchen there are unwashed dishes. An apron hangs from an ancient hook. A perpetual candle burns. A woman squeezes her foot into a shoe that will never fit, but that won't stop her. *Signal a pause in the turmoil.* In the kitchen your grandmother kneads the dough, leaves out the yolk. It is not a sign; though you might read it that way. Great improvisation is in your future. Here is what you know: There are sequential pleats that punctuate every paternal notion. The man who others call father (by any other name) roils in a satin lined coffin, with a heart like lead. Observe the rest of your own life to the letter.

SOGLIA

We dance feverish over our imaginary thresholds. We hold our breath and negotiate for clemency. We like to distract ourselves with continuous interpretation. We should know better by now. Practicalities will never replace desire. Feed the carrion birds by hand. They have built nests like kindling in the eaves of our collective houses. What has been taken will get added on in the end. What has been subtracted will multiple under our perpetual care—we will divide it into enough to feed the lot.

ORMAI

The past is hard to hold and our hands are already full. We boast an inheritance of defiance. Stout and frothy intentions protect our shunned bones. We come from houses where men bent their muscled arms in continuous motion, while breathing the spores that germinated for centuries. Somewhere they still wear the wool that braided their skin through every benign season, on someone else's watch. My father inherited the tradition; similar intent but dressed up in a suit of minerals and glass. I know his respiratory rhythms by heart—we are bonded by a vertical hierarchy established the day I was born. I remain close to the ground, feet on the cold floor, but with a knack for survival, nonetheless. I know how to make plans. *All beauty comes through proportion* and we are all out of sync. I found you all scattered in places, gravitational and with buoyant hearts, hope burning like carbon. There were seasons unlike you've never known but I could tell you about: the nurtured and neglected blastocysts, the tomatoes we let rot on the vine, white sheets, white walls, white nights so stark we became snowblind.

SOMETHING OF OUR LIVES'
WHILE WE WAITED FOR YOU

Some years, in the middle zone, felt like Sundays: bleary and interminable. I took matters into my own hands. I slept dusty and pulsating in drawers of various sizes. I ate the lint in ancient closets, hung myself from a Victorian hook in the dirt floor garage that offered respite. If you think you can't live your life like this, think again. I wanted to coax my mother from her deep slumber that took her far from us. I ironed my father's shirts, like straitjackets, into respectable daily shrouds, an expanse of cotton/ poly blend, stiff with grave disappointment and starch. My sister was a ghost nursing her thumb, while cleaved to my mother's benevolence, pinching the nerves between our eyes at every chance. My brother read a schedule of cancelled trains with a squint and like the rest of us, made optimistic, alternate plans for the future.

DOXOLOGY

Prayers can be anthems to extreme emotions that take a detour. I wear a holy chant like a tattered suit, covering the vulnerability that I will use for another day. Did we pass you on the claustrophobic street? Once I saw you in a dream: you were in many pieces and I gathered your limbs scattered like detritus in a forgotten boneyard. I covered you in a soft flannel, placed you in a box for safekeeping. I lit candles worn to nubs in a basement church, and paid for the privilege to do so. I sang hymns to the creator, abolished all that I might have known before I felt the first stirrings. I swept my arms across the room: let grace enter in her dress of gold wearing a frown. I pin my father's heart to the wall and pray a novena to lost souls; turn the key in the lock. *Walk straight ahead.*

NARRATIVE

Through, not around. Various details that only a daughter-in-law, an outlaw, might be able to cobble into a story. The hatchet with the dull blade nestled under the threadbare chintz cushion to excise memory, to make the dry bones bleed and to keep the blindfolds in place. But here is how we persist: we stop our lady-like mourning, the wringing of our dove-white hands. We leave the life of the novice behind us where we can see her in the rearview mirror as a reminder. We walk through stagnant water, cup the bird in our hands. The anecdotes are gravitational. Open your mouth and find the story has a beginning. *No middle. No end.*

RHIZOMATIC

Your mother smokes her cigarette by the window, laced with frost. Your father nurses a lifelong addiction to folly and chance. Somewhere there is a suitcase packed with all of its contents interchangeable, adjustable to time and place. Sympathetic to the future. Longing is an elemental fraction divided into perpetuity. You belong somewhere but not here. And not there. The heart is in formation. The low thrum through the wall of your chest is not meant to startle and yet it does. A cascade of ornate rage, a gilded bloat. A lifetime of efforts teaching yourself to sing all the songs you know by heart.

REPRISAL

Please go. Words uttered like a benediction, as though time had not curled onto itself and unfurled itself on the floor like the tendril of skin from an apple. Don't we all aim to be elegant in that way? Whose sin was this? The key around your neck and your grandmother waits in her old world worry. You trace the arc of his cheekbones, the filigree webbing of his dark eyes and match them to your own. Eyes closed. Shoulders back. The door ajar. The want of recognition is a noisy cabal with rabid adherents if it is anything at all.

CONTRA

The body is prone to blush when the moon wanes gibbous. Thumb the Bible, trace your finger along the spine of an ancestor. Pick a side. There are ghosts that have been seated at the Sunday dinner table for years, unacknowledged. One can count the souls two by two until they can't anymore. Forks are laid down gently, plates are emptied. When the father closes his eyes and sets his jaw, they will all scatter. The mother scrubs the bones clean in the porcelain sink, then goes out back to cull the persistent seed bed of truth.

SHIBBOLETH

In the time it took to find you, we have settled on sunset standards and fuller lips. We have quelled our jealousy of sacrificial women who know their place and kicked up the dust of everyone who has gone before us. We must deal with knowing they rest uneasy. We have lost layers and languages, but acquired a great respect for natural phenomena. We broke stones when we imagined you. Ran our collective mouths like crooked feet, destined to go without.

ANONDYNE

Everything you might have learned before the clock crowed three times was a threshold concept. What did the unknowing burn into you that you can teach to the deserving? That dark tunnel is a long one, filled with the miasma of what we don't yet know. We follow prescriptives to the letter: Go to bed hungry. Wear the dress with the blue bell sleeves. The one with the gold thread. The one that fits like a glove.

LIGATURE OF LOVE

Promises were made on yesterday's concepts. Once my father told me a story, but it was devoid of details or other recognizable characteristics. My mother chimed in. The words they spoke were 14k gold. I had great hope in what I would find based on what they could never say. I bit my lower lip, drew blood and made a vow to myself like a sharp razor to a quivering throat because I've always been business-like. Somewhere she wove good beginnings, composed salutations into the constellations at night. Somewhere, she brought tenderness into the world devoid of her chromosomes. Here is what we wanted to think: she sheltered in the honeycomb interior of all that might have been possible.

MEANWHILE

He could no longer tell the difference between the sound of the mourning dove, a bottom feeder, or the yellow-eyed owl, a portent of shadowy death. He pinched our nerves. Gave away what he had left, which was nothing. Stared into the middle distance; made covert plans to meet someone halfway.

LIAISE

Who was the first to tell us the lie that the dead can't talk to the living. We have never known the value of things. A year, a month, a day. They pull the cotton wool from their mouths to reduce the numbness and we call it the wind. It was a pattern I had discerned long ago, and it has a lifespan. There has never been a bloodless coup. Alone and separately, we count stars and make plans.

PENTIMENTO

The black and white photographs curled at the edges tell a truncated story. I wrote words to fill in the blanks, imagined scenarios. My father wore a plague of Sundays behind his eyes, locked in a future of melancholy. His father on his back or beside him, reminding him of the old Sicilian conventions of how to behave at weddings, for instance. There are other women, two in particular, who are perpetually at the sink or the stove while other bodies rock in embrace, translate for those who slur phrases in their prospective languages. I put words in their mouths. I want to put spiders on their walls. Shot glasses on their tables. Cigarettes in their ashtrays. I want to cause a necessary break in the monotonous continuum. I want to hold a space for her. For the unknown.

HOW I THOUGHT IT MIGHT HAPPEN

She knocked on the door. A car would sputter away like it had a place to go. Green, blue and red would follow. Her own lack of composure would unnerve her, her knowledge of the culture like wearing the national costume. We would offer gestures which she could spend like currency, should she choose. She would identify our essentials right away, eyes sweeping ancient floorboards to give us our privacy in tense moments. Her father might set his jaw and stare ahead as though he were a monument to all that could go wrong. *A talisman.* Our breeding is highly evolved and has broken records of flight and duration. The evening sky would be starless; silken and purple as it would ever be.

IMPROBABLE

There are several ways to bring home a loved one. Cower at the aching feet of your fate. Pick through the years that seem the densest. *Claim your constellation.* Choose eyes of rubies: keep them fixed on a dying sun.

PARADOXUM

Mother's milk is not a panacea. The scrim of fabric around a father's fedora is not a mark of stability. Who stunted the parental experience? The loose change that he jingled in his pockets alerted hungry dogs, but nothing more. Her anger was tepid. She wore her independence like an ermine collar. Meanwhile uncles everywhere tipped the bottle, licked the foam from smeared glasses in overheated kitchens, lighting each other's cigarettes. The women took offense to everything, guffawed anyway. The children named things by opposites. Tried so hard to still the moving target. Missed every time.

HOLY, HOLY, HOLY

Dulcet tones and a burning hip. There are primacies I was never able to confirm. Virgins may look resplendent in azure chiffon and blush at all the appropriate moments, but they exist in an aural vibrancy in another land, surely not mine. Here everything is devoid of the sheen that makes things more desirable than they really are.

We are afflicted. We sing the names of saints in no particular order and the song still turns in on itself.

Devotion is multifaceted and hides betrayals that are ingenious. It is a faceted diamond, a ray of sun, a corpse flower, a spot of cancer.

Mouth to mouth saliva often tastes like resin. It is the first test of what will last. Warriors will always have a measure of valor that you can count on. The quarantine has been lifted. Cue the ballads, point the shoe. They will be coming for you any time now.

EQUIDAE

Not all theories tell you how to find who you are looking for. Getting through the day is a spiritual act, the blue and yellow lessons it taught me nearly always forgotten on special occasions. I shoved green in a corner and stalked the pink horse all the way to its natural border where it could hang its heavy head and sway on fragile legs. I marked x's in strategic places and hoped to find my way back if only I had half a heart to begin again. The happiness will come either before or after the sadness leaves me bereft at the falling fence. But I am not taking sides. An accelerant with just the right ignition will catch fire simply because it is in its nature to do so.

DERIVE

The locus does its job and intervenes. I reach into my throat and pull forth all of my useless lamentations. We climb the twisted ladder of the double helix, one golden rung at a time. We perch and peer from limbs of the thick rooted trees. An ocean away someone approaches deep function the closer they are to death.

I braided my hands through cobwebbed memory, while you examined the whorls on the tips of your fingers and wondered at the patterns.

We understand what we want, but forget about need that begs on every street corner.

In the gloaming, through all the seasons, I sang

Come to us

> *Come to us.*

And you came.

AFTERWORD

I am seeking, I am striving, I am in it with my whole heart
—Vincent van Gogh

When I was 17 years old, my mother told me that my father had a half-sister. I could not fathom that there was a member of our family, "out there," far from the fold that we did not know. We knew only that she was a year older than my father. No name, no location, no hint of anything.

That my grandfather had another child out there, somewhere was not as much of a surprise as the fact that she remained unknown. This troubled me to the point of distraction. With honesty I can say that for the rest of my life it was a preoccupation of mine, which makes it sound a lot more innocuous than it was: it haunted me. I vowed to find her. Yes, I was curious, but more than that, I wanted to bring her "home," literally and figuratively. While my father and his siblings accepted that, presumably she lived and moved in the world, their often traumatic upbringing and the task at hand—raising their own family's and earning their own livings, precluded spending much, if any time at all, looking for a sister. After all, where would one even begin? I didn't know but I was determined to try.

In the days before the Internet, my search was a passive one. I would think of her a lot. I would scan faces in the small, predominantly Italian-American town in which we live. I would scan faces for certain characteristics, examine temperaments—the line of anger in conversation, for instance that might spring from nowhere at all. I looked in phone books (futile), perked my ears up when I found out that someone of a certain age was adopted. I engaged in endless scenarios, wondering how a young, unmarried woman in the early thirties would do if she found out she was pregnant: be sent away to live with an aunt? Be confined to her house? Live with nuns in a home for unwed mothers? Give the baby up to an orphanage? Remarry, move away and start fresh? The possibilities were endless. I composed rather elaborate scenarios in my head.

The Internet could have made everything potentially easier—except that it didn't. I scanned message boards for identifying characteristics: was someone looking for their birth father's family? Or would my father's half sibling have passed away, already? Would her children be curious enough to look? Has she lived with the pain of rejection her whole life, when he looked into her eyes, the one and only time they shared the same air space—she, only 16 introducing herself, with confidence, young and lovely, to the man who was her father. "Please leave," the only words he spoke to her—--did they haunt? What happened after that?

At times in my life, I felt her close. Those might have been times she was looking herself or wondering if anyone knew about her existence, let alone, be looking for her. She could not assume that just because she knew, everyone knew.

The years passed, and I did all I could to advance the search. I never stopped to think of how delicate the situation really was, or what the ramifications for anyone would actually be. It appears that so many others knew, though. It seemed to be an "open secret" something not unusual in such a close knit community. One month after the birth of what would be his first child, he married my grandmother with impunity, while somewhere, a tiny baby girl was only a month old, and already lacking a father.

At least one person said they would go to the grave with the secret and they did. People are not objects kept for our own amusement. Everyone deserves to know where they come from. She is 85 years of age. She is kind and tenderhearted and funny and loving. She is nothing like what I imagined. She has lived a good life, a life of a loving family, work that was important to her, friends she would do anything for. But she missed us. She told us. And we missed her, too. But we really could not grasp how much until we held her in our arms and looked into her warm, brown eyes.

Because poetry is my way of navigating the world, of making sense of things, where all manner of Italian-American life and my relation to it can be better examined, I wrote these poems *after we found her.*

These poems are not a straight narrative (in the strict sense) about how she came to be in the world, though they do follow a narrative arc nonetheless. I have tried to express *emotional* truth in these poems in the hope that the themes of loss and displacement inherent here will strike a chord that others can identify with, and hopefully find comfort in. My grandfather led an inscrutable life in Sicily, of which we know precious little. He dealt in secrets. Even his name was a pseudonym. I don't think he would have ever dreamed we would find his daughter.

It is never too late for anything. These poems represent my engaged imagination into some details that I could not know.

ACKNOWLEDGMENTS

Thank you to my amazing family both old and new members who believe anything is possible and that miracles do (and did) happen. Thank you to Ancestry DNA. Special thanks to my mother who not only believed, but also patiently watched. *And waited.* Big love to everyone.

ABOUT THE AUTHOR

MICHELLE REALE is an associate professor at Arcadia University. She is the author of 9 collections of poetry, including the forthcoming *Confini: Poems of Refugees in Sicily* (Cervena Barva Press, 2019) and *In the Blink of a Mottled Eye* (Kelsay Books, 2020). She is the Founding and Managing Editor of *Ovunque Siamo: New Italian-American Writing*. She has been twice nominated for a Pushcart Prize.

VIA FOLIOS

A refereed book series dedicated to the culture of Italians and Italian Americans.

MARISA FRASCA. *Wild Fennel*. Vol 137. Poetry. $10
RITA ESPOSITO WATSON. *Italian Kisses*. Vol. 136. Memoir. $14
SARA FRUNER. *Bitter Bites from Sugar Hills*. Vol. 135. Poetry. $12
KATHY CURTO. *Not for Nothing*. Vol. 134. Memoir. $16
JENNIFER MARTELLI. *My Tarantella*. Vol. 133. Poetry. $10
MARIA TERRONE. *At Home in the New World*. Vol. 132. Essays. $16
GIL FAGIANI. *Missing Madonnas*. Vol. 131. Poetry. $14
LEWIS TURCO. *The Sonnetarium*. Vol. 130. Poetry. $12
JOE AMATO. *Samuel Taylor's Hollywood Adventure*. Vol. 129. Novel. $20
BEA TUSIANI. *Con Amore*. Vol. 128. Memoir. $16
MARIA GIURA. *What My Father Taught Me*. Vol. 127. Poetry. $12
STANISLAO PUGLIESE. *A Century of Sinatra*. Vol. 126. Popular Culture. $12
TONY ARDIZZONE. *The Arab's Ox*. Vol. 125. Novel. $18
PHYLLIS CAPELLO. *Packs Small Plays Big*. Vol. 124. Literature.
FRED GARDAPHÉ. *Read 'em and Reap*. Vol. 123. Criticism. $22
JOSEPH A. AMATO. *Diagnostics*. Vol 122. Literature. $12.
DENNIS BARONE. *Second Thoughts*. Vol 121. Poetry. $10
OLIVIA K. CERRONE. *The Hunger Saint*. Vol 120. Novella. $12
GARIBLADI M. LAPOLLA. *Miss Rollins in Love*. Vol 119. Novel. $24
JOSEPH TUSIANI. *A Clarion Call*. Vol 118. Poetry. $16
JOSEPH A. AMATO. *My Three Sicilies*. Vol 117. Poetry & Prose. $17
MARGHERITA COSTA. *Voice of a Virtuosa and Coutesan*. Vol 116. Poetry. $24
NICOLE SANTALUCIA. *Because I Did Not Die*. Vol 115. Poetry. $12
MARK CIABATTARI. *Preludes to History*. Vol 114. Poetry. $12
HELEN BAROLINI. *Visits*. Vol 113. Novel. $22
ERNESTO LIVORNI. *The Fathers' America*. Vol 112. Poetry. $14
MARIO B. MIGNONE. *The Story of My People*. Vol 111. Non-fiction. $17
GEORGE GUIDA. *The Sleeping Gulf*. Vol 110. Poetry. $14
JOEY NICOLETTI. *Reverse Graffiti*. Vol 109. Poetry. $14
GIOSE RIMANELLI. *Il mestiere del furbo*. Vol 108. Criticism. $20
LEWIS TURCO. *The Hero Enkidu*. Vol 107. Poetry. $14
AL TACCONELLI. *Perhaps Fly*. Vol 106. Poetry. $14
RACHEL GUIDO DEVRIES. *A Woman Unknown in Her Bones*. Vol 105. Poetry. $11
BERNARD BRUNO. *A Tear and a Tear in My Heart*. Vol 104. Non-fiction. $20
FELIX STEFANILE. *Songs of the Sparrow*. Vol 103. Poetry. $30
FRANK POLIZZI. *A New Life with Bianca*. Vol 102. Poetry. $10
GIL FAGIANI. *Stone Walls*. Vol 101. Poetry. $14
LOUISE DESALVO. *Casting Off*. Vol 100. Fiction. $22
MARY JO BONA. *I Stop Waiting for You*. Vol 99. Poetry. $12
RACHEL GUIDO DEVRIES. *Stati zitt, Josie*. Vol 98. Children's Literature. $8

GRACE CAVALIERI. *The Mandate of Heaven*. Vol 97. Poetry. $14

MARISA FRASCA. *Via incanto*. Vol 96. Poetry. $12

DOUGLAS GLADSTONE. *Carving a Niche for Himself*. Vol 95. History. $12

MARIA TERRONE. *Eye to Eye*. Vol 94. Poetry. $14

CONSTANCE SANCETTA. *Here in Cerchio*. Vol 93. Local History. $15

MARIA MAZZIOTTI GILLAN. *Ancestors' Song*. Vol 92. Poetry. $14

MICHAEL PARENTI. *Waiting for Yesterday: Pages from a Street Kid's Life*. Vol 90. Memoir. $15

ANNIE LANZILLOTTO. *Schistsong*. Vol 89. Poetry. $15

EMANUEL DI PASQUALE. *Love Lines*. Vol 88. Poetry. $10

CAROSONE & LOGIUDICE. *Our Naked Lives*. Vol 87. Essays. $15

JAMES PERICONI. *Strangers in a Strange Land: A Survey of Italian-Language American Books*.Vol 86. Book History. $24

DANIELA GIOSEFFI. *Escaping La Vita Della Cucina*. Vol 85. Essays. $22

MARIA FAMÀ. *Mystics in the Family*. Vol 84. Poetry. $10

ROSSANA DEL ZIO. *From Bread and Tomatoes to Zuppa di Pesce "Ciambotto"*.Vol. 83. $15

LORENZO DELBOCA. *Polentoni*. Vol 82. Italian Studies. $15

SAMUEL GHELLI. *A Reference Grammar*. Vol 81. Italian Language. $36

ROSS TALARICO. *Sled Run*. Vol 80. Fiction. $15

FRED MISURELLA. *Only Sons*. Vol 79. Fiction. $14

FRANK LENTRICCHIA. *The Portable Lentricchia*. Vol 78. Fiction. $16

RICHARD VETERE. *The Other Colors in a Snow Storm*. Vol 77. Poetry. $10

GARIBALDI LAPOLLA. *Fire in the Flesh*. Vol 76 Fiction & Criticism. $25

GEORGE GUIDA. *The Pope Stories*. Vol 75 Prose. $15

ROBERT VISCUSI. *Ellis Island*. Vol 74. Poetry. $28

ELENA GIANINI BELOTTI. *The Bitter Taste of Strangers Bread*. Vol 73. Fiction. $24

PINO APRILE. *Terroni*. Vol 72. Italian Studies. $20

EMANUEL DI PASQUALE. *Harvest*. Vol 71. Poetry. $10

ROBERT ZWEIG. *Return to Naples*. Vol 70. Memoir. $16

AIROS & CAPPELLI. *Guido*. Vol 69. Italian/American Studies. $12

FRED GARDAPHÉ. *Moustache Pete is Dead! Long Live Moustache Pete!*. Vol 67. Literature/Oral History. $12

PAOLO RUFFILLI. *Dark Room/Camera oscura*. Vol 66. Poetry. $11

HELEN BAROLINI. *Crossing the Alps*. Vol 65. Fiction. $14

COSMO FERRARA. *Profiles of Italian Americans*. Vol 64. Italian Americana. $16

GIL FAGIANI. *Chianti in Connecticut*. Vol 63. Poetry. $10

BASSETTI & D'ACQUINO. *Italic Lessons*. Vol 62. Italian/American Studies. $10

CAVALIERI & PASCARELLI, Eds. *The Poet's Cookbook*. Vol 61. Poetry/Recipes. $12

EMANUEL DI PASQUALE. *Siciliana*. Vol 60. Poetry. $8

NATALIA COSTA, Ed. *Bufalini*. Vol 59. Poetry. $18.

RICHARD VETERE. *Baroque*. Vol 58. Fiction. $18.

LEWIS TURCO. *La Famiglia/The Family*. Vol 57. Memoir. $15

NICK JAMES MILETI. *The Unscrupulous*. Vol 56. Humanities. $20

BASSETTI. ACCOLLA. D'AQUINO. *Italici: An Encounter with Piero Bassetti*. Vol 55. Italian Studies. $8

GIOSE RIMANELLI. *The Three-legged One*. Vol 54. Fiction. $15

CHARLES KLOPP. *Bele Antiche Stòrie*. Vol 53. Criticism. $25

JOSEPH RICAPITO. *Second Wave*. Vol 52. Poetry. $12

GARY MORMINO. *Italians in Florida*. Vol 51. History. $15

GIANFRANCO ANGELUCCI. *Federico F.* Vol 50. Fiction. $15

ANTHONY VALERIO. *The Little Sailor*. Vol 49. Memoir. $9

ROSS TALARICO. *The Reptilian Interludes*. Vol 48. Poetry. $15

RACHEL GUIDO DE VRIES. *Teeny Tiny Tino's Fishing Story*. Vol 47. Children's Literature. $6

EMANUEL DI PASQUALE. *Writing Anew*. Vol 46. Poetry. $15

MARIA FAMÀ. *Looking For Cover*. Vol 45. Poetry. $12

ANTHONY VALERIO. *Toni Cade Bambara's One Sicilian Night*. Vol 44. Poetry. $10

EMANUEL CARNEVALI. *Furnished Rooms*. Vol 43. Poetry. $14

BRENT ADKINS. et al., Ed. *Shifting Borders. Negotiating Places*. Vol 42. Conference. $18

GEORGE GUIDA. *Low Italian*. Vol 41. Poetry. $11

GARDAPHÈ, GIORDANO, TAMBURRI. *Introducing Italian Americana*. Vol 40. Italian/American Studies. $10

DANIELA GIOSEFFI. *Blood Autumn/Autunno di sangue*. Vol 39. Poetry. $15/$25

FRED MISURELLA. *Lies to Live By*. Vol 38. Stories. $15

STEVEN BELLUSCIO. *Constructing a Bibliography*. Vol 37. Italian Americana. $15

ANTHONY JULIAN TAMBURRI, Ed. *Italian Cultural Studies 2002*. Vol 36. Essays. $18

BEA TUSIANI. *con amore*. Vol 35. Memoir. $19

FLAVIA BRIZIO-SKOV, Ed. *Reconstructing Societies in the Aftermath of War*. Vol 34. History. $30

TAMBURRI. et al., Eds. *Italian Cultural Studies 2001*. Vol 33. Essays. $18

ELIZABETH G. MESSINA, Ed. *In Our Own Voices*. Vol 32. Italian/American Studies. $25

STANISLAO G. PUGLIESE. *Desperate Inscriptions*. Vol 31. History. $12

HOSTERT & TAMBURRI, Eds. *Screening Ethnicity*. Vol 30. Italian/American Culture. $25

G. PARATI & B. LAWTON, Eds. *Italian Cultural Studies*. Vol 29. Essays. $18

HELEN BAROLINI. *More Italian Hours*. Vol 28. Fiction. $16

FRANCO NASI, Ed. *Intorno alla Via Emilia*. Vol 27. Culture. $16

ARTHUR L. CLEMENTS. *The Book of Madness & Love*. Vol 26. Poetry. $10

JOHN CASEY, et al. *Imagining Humanity*. Vol 25. Interdisciplinary Studies. $18

ROBERT LIMA. *Sardinia/Sardegna*. Vol 24. Poetry. $10

DANIELA GIOSEFFI. *Going On*. Vol 23. Poetry. $10

ROSS TALARICO. *The Journey Home*. Vol 22. Poetry. $12

EMANUEL DI PASQUALE. *The Silver Lake Love Poems*. Vol 21. Poetry. $7

JOSEPH TUSIANI. *Ethnicity*. Vol 20. Poetry. $12

JENNIFER LAGIER. *Second Class Citizen*. Vol 19. Poetry. $8

FELIX STEFANILE. *The Country of Absence*. Vol 18. Poetry. $9

PHILIP CANNISTRARO. *Blackshirts*. Vol 17. History. $12

LUIGI RUSTICHELLI, Ed. *Seminario sul racconto*. Vol 16. Narrative. $10

LEWIS TURCO. *Shaking the Family Tree*. Vol 15. Memoirs. $9

LUIGI RUSTICHELLI, Ed. *Seminario sulla drammaturgia*. Vol 14. Theater/ Essays. $10

FRED GARDAPHÈ. *Moustache Pete is Dead! Long Live Moustache Pete!*. Vol 13. Oral Literature. $10

JONE GAILLARD CORSI. *Il libretto d'autore. 1860 – 1930*. Vol 12. Criticism. $17

HELEN BAROLINI. *Chiaroscuro: Essays of Identity*. Vol 11. Essays. $15

PICARAZZI & FEINSTEIN, Eds. *An African Harlequin in Milan*. Vol 10. Theater/Essays. $15

JOSEPH RICAPITO. *Florentine Streets & Other Poems*. Vol 9. Poetry. $9

FRED MISURELLA. *Short Time*. Vol 8. Novella. $7

NED CONDINI. *Quartettsatz*. Vol 7. Poetry. $7

ANTHONY JULIAN TAMBURRI, Ed. *Fuori: Essays by Italian/American Lesbiansand Gays*. Vol 6. Essays. $10

ANTONIO GRAMSCI. P. Verdicchio. Trans. & Intro. *The Southern Question*. Vol 5.Social Criticism. $5

DANIELA GIOSEFFI. *Word Wounds & Water Flowers*. Vol 4. Poetry. $8

WILEY FEINSTEIN. *Humility's Deceit: Calvino Reading Ariosto Reading Calvino*. Vol 3. Criticism. $10

PAOLO A. GIORDANO, Ed. *Joseph Tusiani: Poet. Translator. Humanist*. Vol 2. Criticism. $25

ROBERT VISCUSI. *Oration Upon the Most Recent Death of Christopher Columbus*. Vol 1. Poetry.

www.ingramcontent.com/pod-product-compliance
Lightning Source LLC
Chambersburg PA
CBHW020956030426
42339CB00005B/122